# HEALTHY MEDITERRANEAN COOKBOOK

# HEALTHY MEDITERRANEAN COOKBOOK

GOOD FOOD FULL OF ZEST FOR HEALTHY LIVING

Joanna Farrow & Jacqueline Clark

Sebastian Kelly

First published in 1999 by Sebastian Kelly



Produced by Anness Publishing Limited
Hermes House
88–89 Blackfriars Road
London SE1 8HA



ISBN 1 84081 264 8

*Publisher*: Joanna Lorenz
*Senior Cookery Editor*: Linda Fraser
*Designer*: Nigel Partridge
*Illustrations*: Anna Koska
*Photography and styling*: Michelle Garrett, assisted by Dulce Riberio
*Food for photography*: Jacqueline Clark and Joanna Farrow

*Front cover*: Lisa Tai, Designer; Thomas Odulate, Photographer;
Helen Trent, Stylist; Lucy McKelvie, Home Economist

Previously published as *Taste of the Sun* and as part of a larger compendium, *Taste of the Mediterranean*

Printed in Hong Kong/China

1 3 5 7 9 10 8 6 4 2

NOTES
Standard spoon and cup measurements are level.

Medium eggs should be used unless otherwise stated.

# CONTENTS

# Introduction

When thinking of Mediterranean food, it is fresh, sun-ripened fruit, vegetables and herbs which immediately spring to mind. In the open-air markets, which are dotted throughout the region, stall holders pile high their fresh produce and offer it for sale. From Marseilles to Morocco and from Spain to Syria, wonderful arrays of salad greens, garlic, tomatoes, eggplant, zucchini, cherries, peaches, figs and herbs, such as basil and thyme, are temptingly displayed – the hot sun emphasizing the delicious flavors and pungent smells.

It should be no surprise to learn that the Mediterranean diet is a healthy one, since it is based on such fabulous fresh ingredients. Olive oil, which plays a major role in the cooking of the region, contains a high proportion of mono-unsaturated fats and research has proved its beneficial effect on health. The color and flavor of olive oil varies, from the golden Spanish varieties to the deep greens of some Greek, Provençal and Italian oils. Buy the best extra virgin oil to use when the flavor is extra important, as when making salad dressings and mayonnaise-type sauces, such as aïoli and rouille, or for drizzling over roasted vegetables or stirring into pasta. When the oil is simply for sautéing onions or meat, a lighter, and less expensive, olive oil will be just as good, and, especially where the ingredients have more subtle flavors, will not overpower the dish.

The other staple ingredients of the countries surrounding the Mediterranean sea are bread and wine and these, along with olive oil, have been traded throughout the region for hundreds of years. With this trade came an exchange of produce and traditional recipes. Spices and aromatic flavorings were introduced through North Africa and the Arabic countries, and saffron, cloves, chilies, ginger and allspice are still popular all over the Mediterranean, appearing in both sweet and savory dishes. Nuts, such as walnuts, almonds, pistachios and pine nuts are also an ingredient common to many of the countries, and are used in all kinds of dishes, from soups and salads to breads, pastries and desserts.

Perhaps it is the sheer variety of cooking styles that makes Mediterranean cooking so exciting – and inviting. Vegetables, such as peppers, are sometimes sliced into thin sticks to serve as crudités with a flavorful dip, or tossed into a fresh leaf salad, but more often they are roasted to soften them and enhance their flavor, then combined with all manner of other ingredients. In Italy, tomatoes are sun-dried and tossed with tender artichoke hearts in a balsamic vinegar dressing to make a delicious antipasti dish, in Spain, fresh tomatoes and garlic are puréed to make a refreshing chilled soup, while in France, fennel, eggplant and garlic might be roasted around a flavorful corn-fed chicken to delicious effect.

The Mediterranean, of course, abounds with fish and seafood, and a visit to any local restaurant or taverna illustrates how unbeatable this fish, freshly caught and

*LEFT: Glorious green-leafed marigolds shade juicy oranges in a grove near Seville.*

*ABOVE: A basket of ripe figs sits temptingly in the bright Mediterranean sunshine.*

simply cooked, can be: hake gently cooked with olive oil, garlic and fresh parsley; shrimp briefly broiled to accompany a hot chili sauce; and mussels sautéed with garlic and herbs, or stirred into an exotic lobster stew. Meat, too, is prepared in simple flavorful ways; in Spain, lamb is often slow-cooked with red wine, garlic and peppers to make a hearty stew; or it can be formed into delicious meatballs and served Italian-style with melting mozzarella and strips of salty anchovies. Chicken is cooked in myriad ways, but most invitingly with tart lemon slices and lots of garlic to make a rich aromatic stew that in various guises is popular in several countries.

Bread is a staple food throughout the Mediterranean and always accompanies a meal, be it a bowl of soup or a platter of grilled fish. When you consider that it is made using the same basic ingredients, it is remarkable that there is such a variety of flavors and textures.

*BELOW: Freshly cooked Greek bread flavored with olives; simple but delicious fare.*

There are Italian soft breads, cooked simply with a topping of sea salt, or flavored with sun-dried tomatoes and herbs, gorgeous Greek olive breads and delicious unleavened pita breads, easy to buy ready-made, which are often used instead of knives and forks; when slit, the empty pocket makes a perfect container for salads, bean dishes and meats.

A peep in the display cabinets of any patisserie, confectioner or coffee house just about anywhere in the Mediterranean will reveal a feast of sweet treats. From highly decorated gâteaux to delicate cakes, cookies and tarts, all Mediterranean sweets thrive on an abundance of fabulous flavors. Home-cooked desserts take full advantage of the glorious abundance of fresh fruits. For a special occasion, a colorful selection of seasonal fruits, such as peaches, apricots, melons and cherries make a stunning finale. Fresh fruits, such as figs, can be poached in a honey-sweetened syrup to serve with cream, and tart oranges can be turned into a refreshing sherbet and served French-style in the fruit shell. Dates are popular throughout the region: combined with an almond cream filling encased in crisp pastry, this medley of Mediterranean flavors makes a mouthwatering tart.

Mediterranean food is simple to cook, delicious and healthy. In this book, we have collected just a few of the vast repertoire of dishes from around the region, some traditional and others more contemporary, using classic ingredients, but creating something new – we hope that you enjoy cooking them and that we will bring a true Mediterranean flavor to your kitchen.

# Soups and Appetizers

*Across the Mediterranean there is a splendid array of soups and appetizers to be enjoyed throughout the year that make the most of the abundance of fresh vegetables.*

# ROASTED PEPPER ANTIPASTO

*Jars of Italian mixed peppers in olive oil are now a common sight in many supermarkets. None, however, can compete with this colorful, freshly made version, perfect as an appetizer on its own, or with some Italian salamis and cold meats.*

*3 red bell peppers*
*2 yellow or orange bell peppers*
*2 green bell peppers*
*½ cup sun-dried tomatoes in oil, drained*
*2 tablespoons balsamic vinegar*
*5 tablespoons olive oil*
*few drops of chili sauce*
*4 canned artichoke hearts, drained and sliced*
*1 garlic clove, sliced*
*salt and ground black pepper*
*basil leaves, to garnish*

SERVES 6

1 Preheat the oven to 400°F. Lightly oil a foil-lined baking sheet and place the whole peppers on the foil. Bake for about 45 minutes until beginning to char. Remove from the oven, cover with a dish towel and allow to cool for 5 minutes.

2 Slice the sun-dried tomatoes. Remove the core and seeds from the peppers and peel away the skins. Slice each pepper into thick strips.

3 Beat together the vinegar, oil and chili sauce, then season with a little salt and pepper.

4 Toss the peppers with the sliced artichokes, tomatoes and garlic. Pour on the dressing and scatter with the basil leaves.

# FALAFEL

*In North Africa these spicy fritters are made using dried fava beans, but chickpeas are much easier to buy. They are lovely served as a snack with garlicky yogurt or stuffed into warmed pita bread.*

*¾ cup dried chickpeas*
*1 large onion, coarsely chopped*
*2 garlic cloves, coarsely chopped*
*4 tablespoons coarsely chopped parsley*
*1 teaspoon cumin seeds, crushed*
*1 teaspoon coriander seeds, crushed*
*½ teaspoon baking powder*
*salt and ground black pepper*
*oil for deep frying*
*pita bread, salad and yogurt, to serve*

SERVES 4

1 Put the chickpeas in a bowl with plenty of cold water. Allow to soak overnight.

2 Drain the chickpeas and cover with water in a pan. Bring to a boil. Boil rapidly for 10 minutes. Reduce the heat and simmer for about 1 hour until soft. Drain.

3 Place in a food processor with the onion, garlic, parsley, cumin, coriander and baking powder. Add salt and pepper to taste. Process until the mixture forms a firm paste.

4 Shape the mixture into walnut-size balls and flatten them slightly. In a deep pan, heat 2 inches oil until a little of the mixture sizzles on the surface. Fry the falafel in batches until golden. Drain on paper towels and keep hot while frying the remainder. Serve warm, in pita bread, with salad and yogurt.

# TAPENADE AND HERB AIOLI WITH SUMMER VEGETABLES

*A beautiful platter of salad vegetables served with one or two interesting sauces makes a thoroughly delicious and informal appetizer. This colorful French dish is perfect for entertaining as it can be prepared in advance.*

FOR THE TAPENADE
*1½ cups pitted black olives*
*2-ounce can anchovy fillets, drained*
*2 tablespoons capers*
*½ cup olive oil*
*finely grated rind of 1 lemon*
*1 tablespoon brandy (optional)*
*ground black pepper*

FOR THE HERB AIOLI
*2 egg yolks*
*1 teaspoon Dijon mustard*
*2 teaspoons white wine vinegar*
*1 cup light olive oil*
*3 tablespoons chopped mixed fresh herbs, such as chervil, parsley or tarragon*
*2 tablespoons chopped watercress*
*5 garlic cloves, crushed*
*salt and ground black pepper*

TO SERVE
*2 red bell peppers, seeded and cut into wide strips*
*2 tablespoons olive oil*
*8 ounces new potatoes*
*4 ounces green beans*
*8 ounces baby carrots*
*8 ounces young asparagus*
*12 quail's eggs (optional)*
*fresh herbs, to garnish*
*coarse salt for sprinkling*

SERVES 6

1 To make the tapenade, finely chop the olives, anchovies and capers and beat together with the oil, lemon rind and brandy if using. (Alternatively, lightly process the ingredients in a blender or food processor, scraping down the mixture from the sides of the bowl if necessary.)

2 Season with pepper and blend in a little more oil if the mixture is very dry. Transfer to a serving dish.

3 To make the aïoli, beat together the egg yolks, mustard and vinegar. Gradually blend in the oil, a trickle at a time, whisking well after each addition until thick and smooth. Season with salt and pepper to taste, adding a little more vinegar if the aïoli tastes bland.

4 Stir in the mixed herbs, watercress and garlic, then transfer to a serving dish. Cover and put in the fridge.

5 Put the peppers on a foil-lined broiler rack and brush with the oil. Broil under high heat until just beginning to char.

6 Cook the potatoes in a large pan of boiling, salted water until just tender. Add the beans and carrots and cook for 1 minute. Add the asparagus and cook for another 30 seconds. Drain the vegetables.

7 Cook the quail's eggs in boiling water for 2 minutes. Drain and remove half of each shell.

8 Arrange all the vegetables, eggs and sauces on a serving platter. Garnish with fresh herbs and serve with coarse salt for sprinkling.

COOK'S TIP
Keep any leftover sauces for serving with salads. The tapenade is also delicious tossed with pasta or spread onto warm toast.

# Broiled Vegetable Terrine

*A colorful, layered terrine, using all the vegetables associated with the Mediterranean.*

*2 large red bell peppers, quartered, cored and seeded*
*2 large yellow bell peppers, quartered, cored and seeded*
*1 large eggplant, sliced lengthwise*
*2 large zucchini, sliced lengthwise*
*6 tablespoons olive oil*
*1 large red onion, thinly sliced*
*½ cup raisins*
*1 tablespoon tomato paste*
*1 tablespoon red wine vinegar*
*1⅔ cups tomato juice*
*2 tablespoons powdered gelatin*
*fresh basil leaves, to garnish*

For the Dressing
*6 tablespoons extra virgin olive oil*
*2 tablespoons red wine vinegar*
*salt and ground black pepper*

Serves 6

1 Place the prepared red and yellow peppers skin side up under a hot broiler and cook until the skins are blackened. Transfer to a bowl and cover with a plate. Allow to cool.

2 Arrange the eggplant and zucchini slices on separate baking sheets. Brush them with a little oil and cook under the broiler, turning occasionally, until tender and golden.

3 Heat the remaining olive oil in a frying pan, and add the sliced onion, raisins, tomato paste and red wine vinegar. Cook gently until soft and syrupy. Let the mixture cool in the frying pan.

4 Line a 7½-cup terrine with plastic wrap (it helps to lightly oil the terrine first), leaving a little hanging over the sides.

5 Pour half the tomato juice into a saucepan, and sprinkle with the gelatin. Dissolve gently over low heat, stirring.

6 Place a layer of red peppers in the bottom of the terrine, and pour in enough of the tomato juice with gelatin to cover. Continue layering the eggplant, zucchini, yellow peppers and onion mixture, finishing with another layer of red peppers. Pour tomato juice over each layer of vegetables.

7 Add the remaining tomato juice to any left in the pan, and pour into the terrine. Give it a sharp tap, to disperse the juice. Cover the terrine and chill until set.

8 To make the dressing, whisk together the oil and vinegar, and season. Turn out the terrine and remove the plastic wrap. Serve in thick slices, drizzled with dressing. Garnish with basil leaves.

# CHILLED ALMOND SOUP

*Unless you want to spend time pounding the ingredients for this dish by hand, a food processor is essential. Then you'll find that this Spanish soup is very simple to make and refreshing to eat on a hot day.*

*4 ounces fresh white bread*
*1 cup blanched almonds*
*2 garlic cloves, sliced*
*5 tablespoons olive oil*
*1½ tablespoons sherry vinegar*
*salt and ground black pepper*
*toasted flaked almonds and seedless green and black grapes, halved and skinned, to garnish*

SERVES 6

1 Break the bread into a bowl and pour on ⅔ cup cold water. Let sit for 5 minutes.

2 Put the almonds and garlic in a blender or food processor and process until very finely ground. Blend in the soaked white bread.

3 Gradually add the olive oil until the mixture forms a smooth paste. Add the sherry vinegar then 2½ cups cold water and process until smooth.

4 Transfer to a bowl and season with salt and pepper, adding a little more water if the soup is very thick. Chill for at least 2–3 hours.

5 Ladle the soup into bowls and scatter with the toasted almonds and skinned grapes.

# GAZPACHO

*There are many versions of this refreshingly chilled, pungent soup from southern Spain. All contain an intense blend of tomatoes, peppers, cucumber and garlic; perfect on a hot summer's evening.*

*2 pounds ripe tomatoes*
*1 cucumber*
*2 red bell peppers, seeded and coarsely chopped*
*2 garlic cloves, crushed*
*3 cups fresh white bread crumbs*
*2 tablespoons white wine vinegar*
*2 tablespoons sun-dried tomato paste*
*6 tablespoons olive oil*
*salt and ground black pepper*

TO FINISH

*1 slice white bread, crust removed and cut into cubes*
*2 tablespoons olive oil*
*6–12 ice cubes*
*small bowl of mixed chopped garnishes, such as tomato, cucumber, red onion, hard-boiled egg and flat leaf parsley or tarragon leaves*

SERVES 6

COOK'S TIP

The sun-dried tomato paste has been added to accentuate the flavor of the tomatoes. You might not need this if you use a really flavorful variety.

1 Plunge the tomatoes into boiling water for 30 seconds, then refresh in cold water. Peel away the skins and quarter. Peel and coarsely chop the cucumber. Mix the tomatoes and cucumber in a bowl with the peppers, garlic, bread crumbs, vinegar, tomato paste and olive oil and season lightly with salt and pepper.

2 Process half the mixture in a blender or food processor until fairly smooth. Process the remaining mixture and mix with the first.

3 Check the seasoning and add a little cold water if the soup is too thick. Chill for several hours.

4 To finish, fry the bread in the oil until golden. Spoon the soup into bowls, adding one or two ice cubes to each. Serve accompanied by the croûtons and garnishes.

# SEAFOOD SOUP WITH ROUILLE

*This is a really chunky, aromatic mixed fish soup from France, flavored with plenty of saffron and herbs. Rouille, a fiery hot paste, is served separately for everyone to swirl into their soup to flavor.*

*3 snapper or red mullet, scaled and gutted*
*12 large shrimp*
*1½ pounds white fish, such as cod, haddock, halibut or monkfish*
*8 ounces fresh mussels*
*1 onion, quartered*
*1 teaspoon saffron strands*
*5 tablespoons olive oil*
*1 fennel bulb, coarsely chopped*
*4 garlic cloves, crushed*
*3 strips pared orange rind*
*4 thyme sprigs*
*1½ pounds tomatoes or 14-ounce can chopped tomatoes*
*2 tablespoons sun-dried tomato paste*
*3 bay leaves*
*salt and ground black pepper*

FOR THE ROUILLE
*1 red bell pepper, seeded and coarsely chopped*
*1 red chili, seeded and sliced*
*2 garlic cloves, chopped*
*5 tablespoons olive oil*
*¼ cup fresh bread crumbs*

SERVES 6

1 To make the rouille, process the pepper, chili, garlic, oil and bread crumbs in a blender or food processor until smooth. Transfer to a serving dish and chill.

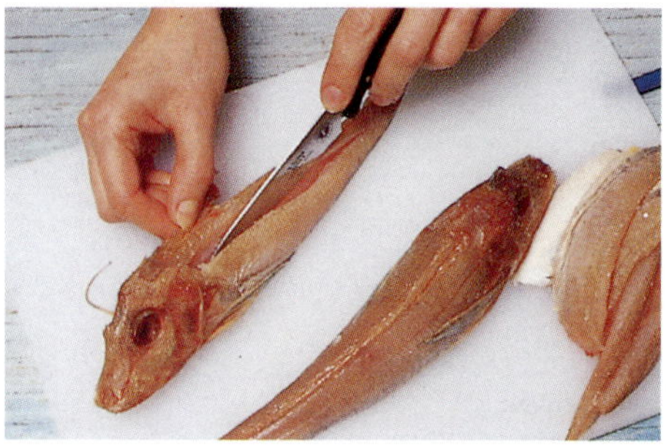

2 Fillet the snapper or mullet by cutting away the flesh from either side of the backbone, reserving the heads and bones. Cut the fillets into small chunks. Shell half the shrimp and reserve the trimmings for the stock. Skin the white fish, discarding any bones, and cut into chunks. Thoroughly scrub the mussels, discarding any that are damaged or any open ones that do not close when tapped with a knife.

3 Put the fish and shrimp trimmings in a large saucepan with the onion and about 5 cups water. Bring to a boil, then simmer gently for 30 minutes. Cool slightly and strain.

4 Soak the saffron in 1 tablespoon boiling water. Heat about 2 tablespoons of the oil in a large sauté pan or saucepan. Add the snapper or mullet and white fish and fry over high heat for 1 minute. Drain.

5 Heat the remaining oil and fry the fennel, garlic, orange rind and thyme until beginning to color. Make up the strained stock to about 5 cups with water.

COOK'S TIP
To save time, order the fish and ask the fish seller to fillet the gurnard or mullet for you.

6 If using fresh tomatoes, plunge them into boiling water for 30 seconds, then refresh in cold water. Peel and chop. Add the stock to the pan with the saffron, tomatoes, tomato paste and bay leaves. Season, bring almost to a boil, then simmer gently, covered, for 20 minutes.

7 Stir in the snapper or mullet, white fish and shrimp and add the mussels. Cover the pan and cook for 3–4 minutes. Discard any mussels that do not open. Serve the soup hot with the rouille.

# PISTOU

*A delicious vegetable soup from Nice in the south of France, served with a sun-dried tomato pesto, and fresh Parmesan cheese.*

*1 zucchini, diced*
*1 small potato, diced*
*1 shallot, chopped*
*1 carrot, diced*
*8-ounce can chopped tomatoes*
*5 cups vegetable stock*
*2 ounces green beans, cut into ½-inch pieces*
*½ cup frozen petits pois*
*½ cup small pasta shapes*
*4–6 tablespoons homemade or bought pesto*
*1 tablespoon sun-dried tomato paste*
*salt and ground black pepper*
*freshly grated Parmesan cheese, to serve*

SERVES 4–6

1. Place the zucchini, potato, shallot, carrot and tomatoes in a large pan. Add the vegetable stock and season with salt and pepper. Bring to a boil, then cover and simmer for 20 minutes.

2. Add the green beans, petits pois and pasta. Cook for another 10 minutes, until the pasta is tender. Adjust the seasoning.

3. Ladle the soup into individual bowls. Mix together the pesto and sun-dried tomato paste, and stir a spoonful into each serving. Serve with grated Parmesan cheese to sprinkle into each bowl.

# Chilled Tomato and Sweet Bell Pepper Soup

*A recipe inspired by the Spanish gazpacho, the difference being that this soup is cooked first, and then chilled.*

*2 red bell peppers, halved, cored and seeded*
*3 tablespoons olive oil*
*1 onion, finely chopped*
*2 garlic cloves, crushed*
*1½ pounds ripe well-flavored tomatoes*
*⅔ cup red wine*
*2½ cups chicken stock*
*salt and ground black pepper*
*snipped fresh chives, to garnish*

For the croutons
*2 slices white bread, crusts removed*
*4 tablespoons olive oil*

Serves 4

1 Cut each pepper half into quarters. Place skin side up on a broiler rack and cook until the skins have charred. Transfer to a bowl and cover with a plate.

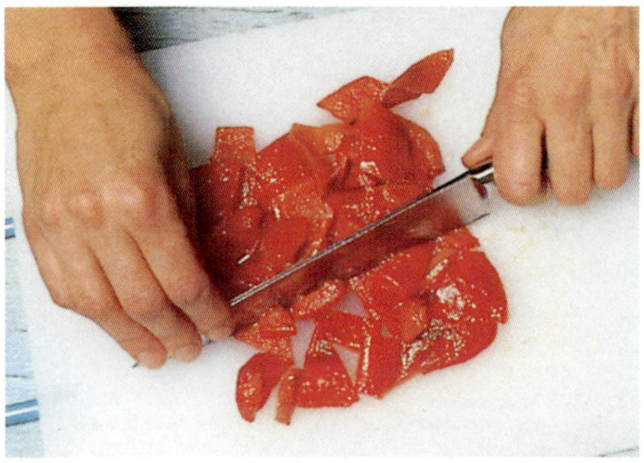

2 Heat the oil in a large pan. Add the onion and garlic and cook until soft. Meanwhile, remove the skin from the peppers and coarsely chop them. Cut the tomatoes into chunks.

3 Add the peppers and tomatoes to the pan, then cover and cook gently for 10 minutes. Add the wine and cook for another 5 minutes, then add the stock and salt and pepper and continue to simmer for 20 minutes.

4 To make the croûtons, cut the bread into cubes. Heat the oil in a small frying pan, add the bread and fry until golden. Drain on paper towels and store in an airtight box.

5 Process the soup in a blender or food processor until smooth. Pour into a clean glass or ceramic bowl and let cool thoroughly before chilling in the fridge for at least 3 hours. When the soup is cold, season to taste.

6 Serve the soup in bowls, topped with the croûtons and garnished with snipped chives.

# RIBOLLITA

*Ribollita is rather like minestrone, but includes beans instead of pasta. In Italy it is traditionally served ladled over bread and a rich green vegetable, although you could omit this for a lighter version.*

*3 tablespoons olive oil*
*2 onions, chopped*
*2 carrots, sliced*
*4 garlic cloves, crushed*
*2 celery stalks, thinly sliced*
*1 fennel bulb, trimmed and chopped*
*2 large zucchini, thinly sliced*
*14-ounce can chopped tomatoes*
*2 tablespoons homemade or bought pesto*
*3¾ cups vegetable stock*
*14-ounce can navy or pinto beans, drained*
*salt and ground black pepper*

To Finish
*1 pound young spinach*
*1 tablespoon extra virgin olive oil, plus extra for drizzling*
*6–8 slices white bread*
*Parmesan cheese shavings*

Serves 6–8

Variation
Use other dark greens, such as chard or cabbage instead of the spinach; shred and cook until tender.

1 Heat the oil in a large saucepan. Add the onions, carrots, garlic, celery and fennel and fry gently for 10 minutes. Add the zucchini and fry for another 2 minutes.

2 Add the chopped tomatoes, pesto, stock and beans and bring to a boil. Reduce the heat, cover and simmer gently for 25–30 minutes, until the vegetables are completely tender. Season with salt and pepper to taste.

3 To serve, fry the spinach in the oil for 2 minutes or until wilted. Spoon on the bread in soup bowls, then ladle the soup on the spinach. Serve with extra olive oil for drizzling onto the soup and Parmesan cheese to sprinkle on top.

# SPANISH GARLIC SOUP

*This is a simple and satisfying soup, made with one of the most popular ingredients in the Mediterranean – garlic!*

*2 tablespoons olive oil*
*4 large garlic cloves, peeled*
*4 slices French bread, ¼-inch thick*
*1 tablespoon paprika*
*4 cups beef stock*
*¼ teaspoon ground cumin*
*pinch of saffron strands*
*4 eggs*
*salt and ground black pepper*
*chopped fresh parsley, to garnish*

SERVES 4

1 Preheat the oven to 450°F. Heat the oil in a large pan. Add the whole garlic cloves and cook for a minute or two until golden. Remove and set aside. Fry the bread in the oil until golden, then set aside.

2 Add the paprika to the pan, and fry for a few seconds. Stir in the beef stock, cumin and saffron, then add the reserved garlic, crushing the cloves with the back of a wooden spoon. Season with salt and pepper then cook for about 5 minutes.

3 Ladle the soup into four ovenproof bowls and break an egg into each. Place the slices of fried bread on top of the egg and place in the oven for about 3–4 minutes, until the eggs are set. Sprinkle with parsley and serve at once.

# VEGETABLES AND VEGETARIAN DISHES

*Vegetables take pride of place on the Mediterranean table; with such a treasure trove of vegetables ranging from the exotic eggplant to the humble potato this is no wonder.*

# BROILED EGGPLANT PARCELS

*These are delicious little Italian bundles of tomatoes, mozzarella cheese and basil, wrapped in slices of eggplant.*

*2 large, long eggplant*
*8 ounces mozzarella cheese*
*2 plum tomatoes*
*16 large basil leaves*
*salt and ground black pepper*
*2 tablespoons olive oil*

FOR THE DRESSING
*4 tablespoons olive oil*
*1 teaspoon balsamic vinegar*
*1 tablespoon sun-dried tomato paste*
*1 tablespoon lemon juice*

FOR THE GARNISH
*2 tablespoons toasted pine nuts*
*torn basil leaves*

SERVES 4

1 Remove the stalks from the eggplant and cut the eggplant lengthwise into thin slices – the aim is to get 16 slices in total, disregarding the first and last slices (each about ¼-inch thick). (If you have a mandoline, it will cut perfect, even slices for you, otherwise use a long-bladed, sharp knife.)

2 Bring a large pan of salted water to a boil and cook the eggplant slices for about 2 minutes, until just softened. Drain the sliced eggplant, then dry on paper towels.

3 Cut the mozzarella cheese into eight slices. Cut each tomato into eight slices, not counting the first and last slices.

4 Take two eggplant slices and place on a flameproof tray or dish, in a cross (*left*). Place a slice of tomato in the center, season with salt and pepper, then add a basil leaf, followed by a slice of mozzarella, another basil leaf, a slice of tomato and more seasoning.

5 Fold the ends of the eggplant slices around the mozzarella and tomato filling to make a neat parcel (*left*). Repeat with the rest of the assembled ingredients to make eight parcels. Chill the parcels for about 20 minutes.

6 To make the tomato dressing, whisk together the olive oil, vinegar, sun-dried tomato paste and lemon juice. Season to taste.

7 Preheat the broiler. Brush the parcels with olive oil and cook for about 5 minutes on each side, until golden. Serve hot, with the dressing, sprinkled with pine nuts and basil.

# POLPETTES

*Delicious little fried morsels of potato and Greek feta cheese, flavored with dill and lemon juice.*

*1¼ pounds potatoes*
*4 ounces feta cheese*
*4 scallions, chopped*
*3 tablespoons chopped fresh dill*
*1 egg, beaten*
*1 tablespoon lemon juice*
*salt and ground black pepper*
*flour for dredging*
*3 tablespoons olive oil*

SERVES 4

1 Boil the potatoes in their skins in lightly salted water until soft. Drain, then peel while still warm. Place in a bowl and mash. Crumble the feta cheese into the potatoes and add the scallions, dill, egg and lemon juice and season with salt and pepper. (The cheese is salty, so taste before you add salt.) Stir well.

2 Cover the mixture and chill until firm. Divide the mixture into walnut-size balls, then flatten them slightly. Dredge with flour. Heat the oil in a frying pan and fry the polpettes until golden brown on each side. Drain on paper towels and serve immediately.

# SPINACH AND RICOTTA GNOCCHI

*The success of this Italian dish lies in not overworking the mixture, to achieve delicious, light mouthfuls.*

*2 pounds fresh spinach*
*1½ cups ricotta cheese*
*4 tablespoons freshly grated Parmesan cheese*
*3 eggs, beaten*
*¼ teaspoon grated nutmeg*
*3–4 tablespoons flour*
*½ cup butter, melted*
*salt and ground black pepper*
*freshly grated Parmesan cheese, to serve*

SERVES 4

1 Place the spinach in a large pan and cook for 5 minutes, until wilted. Allow to cool, then squeeze the spinach as dry as possible. Process in a blender or food processor, then transfer to a bowl.

2 Add the ricotta, Parmesan, eggs and nutmeg. Season with salt and pepper and mix together. Add enough flour to make the mixture into a soft dough. Using your hands, shape the mixture into 3-inch sausages, then dust lightly with flour.

3 Bring a large pan of salted water to a boil. Gently slide the gnocchi into the water and cook for 1–2 minutes, until they float to the surface. Remove the gnocchi with a slotted spoon and transfer to a warmed dish. Pour on the melted butter and sprinkle with Parmesan cheese. Serve immediately.

# STUFFED TOMATOES AND PEPPERS

*Colorful peppers and tomatoes make perfect containers for various meat and vegetable stuffings. This rice and herb version uses typically Greek ingredients.*

### VARIATION

Small eggplant or large zucchini also make good vegetables for stuffing. Halve and scoop out the centers of the vegetables, then oil the vegetable shells and bake for about 15 minutes. Chop the centers, fry for 2–3 minutes to soften and add to the stuffing mixture. Fill the eggplant or zucchini shells with the stuffing and bake as for the peppers and tomatoes.

*2 large ripe tomatoes*
*1 green bell pepper*
*1 yellow or orange bell pepper*
*4 tablespoons olive oil, plus extra for sprinkling*
*2 onions, chopped*
*2 garlic cloves, crushed*
*½ cup blanched almonds, chopped*
*scant ½ cup long grain rice, boiled and drained*
*½ ounce mint, roughly chopped*
*½ ounce parsley, coarsely chopped*
*2 tablespoons golden raisins*
*3 tablespoons ground almonds*
*salt and ground black pepper*
*chopped mixed herbs, to garnish*

SERVES 4

1 Preheat the oven to 375°F. Cut the tomatoes in half and scoop out the pulp and seeds using a teaspoon. Leave the tomatoes to drain on paper towels with cut sides down. Coarsely chop the tomato pulp and seeds and set aside.

2 Halve the peppers, leaving the cores intact. Scoop out the seeds. Brush the peppers with 1 tablespoon of the oil and bake on a baking sheet for 15 minutes. Place the peppers and tomatoes in a shallow ovenproof dish and season with salt and pepper.

3 Fry the onions in the remaining oil for 5 minutes. Add the garlic and chopped almonds and fry for another minute.

4 Remove the pan from the heat and stir in the rice, chopped tomatoes, mint, parsley and golden raisins. Season well with salt and pepper and spoon the mixture into the tomatoes and peppers.

5 Pour ⅔ cup boiling water around the tomatoes and peppers and bake, uncovered, for 20 minutes. Scatter with the ground almonds and sprinkle with a little extra olive oil. Return to the oven and bake for 20 minutes more, or until turning golden. Serve garnished with fresh herbs.

# ZUCCHINI FRITTERS WITH PISTOU

*These delicious fritters are a specialty of Southern France. The pistou sauce provides a lovely contrast in flavor, but you could substitute other sauces, like a garlicky tomato one or a herb dressing*

FOR THE PISTOU
*½ ounce basil leaves*
*4 garlic cloves, crushed*
*1 cup grated Parmesan cheese*
*finely grated rind of 1 lemon*
*⅔ cup olive oil*

FOR THE FRITTERS
*1 pound zucchini, grated*
*⅔ cup flour*
*1 egg, separated*
*1 tablespoon olive oil*
*oil for shallow frying*
*salt and ground black pepper*

SERVES 4

1. To make the pistou, crush the basil leaves and garlic with a pestle and mortar to make a fairly fine paste. Transfer the paste to a bowl and stir in the grated cheese and lemon rind. Gradually blend in the oil, a little at a time, until combined, then transfer to a small serving dish.

2. To make the fritters, put the grated zucchini in a strainer over a bowl and sprinkle with plenty of salt. Leave for 1 hour, then rinse thoroughly. Dry well on paper towels.

3. Sift the flour into a bowl and make a well in the center, then add the egg yolk and oil. Measure 5 tablespoons water and add a little to the bowl.

4. Whisk the egg yolk and oil, gradually incorporating the flour and water to make a smooth batter. Season and let sit for 30 minutes.

5. Stir the zucchini into the batter. Whisk the egg white until stiff, then fold into the batter.

6. Heat ½ inch of oil in a frying pan. Add spoonfuls of batter to the oil and fry for 2 minutes until golden. Drain the fritters on paper towels and keep warm while frying the rest. Serve with the sauce.

# RATATOUILLE

*A highly versatile vegetable stew from Provence. Ratatouille is delicious hot or cold, on its own or with eggs, pasta, fish or meat – particularly roast lamb.*

*2 pounds ripe, well-flavored tomatoes*
*½ cup olive oil*
*2 onions, thinly sliced*
*2 red bell peppers, seeded and cut into chunks*
*1 yellow or orange bell pepper, seeded and cut into chunks*
*1 large eggplant, cut into chunks*
*2 zucchini, cut into thick slices*
*4 garlic cloves, crushed*
*2 bay leaves*
*1 tablespoon chopped young thyme*
*salt and ground black pepper*

SERVES 6

1 Plunge the tomatoes into boiling water for 30 seconds, then refresh in cold water. Peel away the skins and chop coarsely.

2 Heat a little of the oil in a large, heavy-based pan and fry the onions for 5 minutes. Add the peppers and fry for another 2 minutes. Drain. Add the eggplant and more oil and fry gently for 5 minutes. Add the remaining oil and zucchini and fry for 3 minutes. Drain.

3 Add the garlic and tomatoes to the pan with the bay leaves and thyme and a little salt and pepper. Cook gently until the tomatoes have softened and are turning pulpy.

4 Return all the vegetables to the pan and cook gently, stirring frequently, for about 15 minutes, until fairly pulpy but retaining a little texture. Season with more salt and pepper to taste.

COOK'S TIP

There are no specific quantities for the vegetables when making ratatouille, so you can, to a large extent, vary the quantities and types of vegetables depending on what you have in the fridge. If the tomatoes are a little tasteless, add 2–3 tablespoons tomato paste and a dash of sugar to the mixture along with the tomatoes.

# SPINACH WITH RAISINS AND PINE NUTS

*Raisins and pine nuts are frequent partners in Spanish recipes. Here, tossed with wilted spinach and croûtons, they make a delicious snack or main meal accompaniment.*

*⅓ cup raisins*
*1 thick slice crusty white bread*
*3 tablespoons olive oil*
*⅓ cup pine nuts*
*1¼ pounds young spinach, stalks removed*
*2 garlic cloves, crushed*
*salt and ground black pepper*

SERVES 4

1 Put the raisins in a small bowl with boiling water and allow to soak for 10 minutes. Drain.

2 Cut the bread into cubes and discard the crusts. Heat 2 tablespoons of the oil and fry the bread until golden. Drain.

3 Heat the remaining oil in the pan. Fry the pine nuts until beginning to color. Add the spinach and garlic and cook quickly, turning the spinach until it has just wilted.

4 Toss in the raisins and season lightly with salt and pepper. Transfer to a warmed serving dish. Scatter with croûtons and serve hot.

VARIATION

Use Swiss chard or beet greens instead of the spinach, cooking them a little longer.

# SPICED TURNIPS WITH SPINACH AND TOMATOES

*Sweet baby turnips, tender spinach and ripe tomatoes make tempting partners in this simple Eastern Mediterranean vegetable stew.*

*1 pound plum or other well-flavored tomatoes*
*4 tablespoons olive oil*
*2 onions, sliced*
*1 pound baby turnips, peeled*
*1 teaspoon paprika*
*½ teaspoon sugar*
*4 tablespoons chopped fresh cilantro*
*1 pound fresh young spinach, stalks removed*
*salt and ground black pepper*

SERVES 6

1 Plunge the tomatoes into a bowl of boiling water for 30 seconds, then refresh in a bowl of cold water. Peel away the tomato skins and chop coarsely. Heat the olive oil in a large frying pan or sauté pan and fry the onion slices for about 5 minutes until golden.

2 Add the baby turnips, tomatoes and paprika to the pan with 4 tablespoons water and cook until the tomatoes are pulpy. Cover with a lid and continue cooking until the baby turnips have softened.

3 Stir in the sugar and cilantro, then add the spinach and a little salt and pepper and cook for another 2–3 minutes until the spinach has wilted. Serve warm or cold.

# MUSHROOM AND PESTO PIZZA

*Home-made Italian-style pizzas are a little time-consuming to make but the results are well worth the effort.*

FOR THE PIZZA BASE
*3 cups strong flour*
*¼ teaspoon salt*
*½ ounce fast-rising dried yeast*
*1 tablespoon olive oil*

FOR THE FILLING
*2 ounces dried porcini mushrooms*
*¾ cup fresh basil*
*⅓ cup pine nuts*
*1½ ounces Parmesan cheese, thinly sliced*
*7 tablespoons olive oil*
*2 onions, thinly sliced*
*8 ounces cremini mushrooms, sliced*
*salt and ground black pepper*

SERVES 4

1 To make the pizza base, put the flour in a bowl with the salt, dried yeast and olive oil. Add 1 cup hand-hot water and mix to a dough using a round-bladed knife.

2 Turn onto a work surface and knead for 5 minutes until smooth. Place in a clean bowl, cover with plastic wrap and let rise in a warm place until doubled in bulk.

3 Meanwhile, make the filling. Soak the dried mushrooms in hot water for 20 minutes. Place the basil, pine nuts, Parmesan and 5 tablespoons of the olive oil in a blender or food processor and process to make a smooth paste. Set the paste aside.

4 Fry the onions in the remaining olive oil for 3–4 minutes until beginning to color. Add the cremini mushrooms and fry for 2 minutes. Stir in the drained porcini mushrooms and season lightly.

5 Preheat the oven to 425°F. Lightly grease a large baking sheet. Turn the pizza dough onto a floured surface and roll out to a 12-inch circle. Place the dough on the baking sheet.

6 Spread the pesto mixture to within ½ inch of the edges. Spread the mushroom mixture on top.

7 Bake the pizza for 35–40 minutes until risen and golden.

# PAPPARDELLE WITH OLIVE AND CAPER PASTE

*This homemade pasta is flavored with sun-dried tomato paste. The results are well worth the effort, but bought pasta can be substituted for a really quick supper dish.*

FOR THE PASTA
*2½ cups white flour*
*¼ teaspoon salt*
*3 eggs*
*3 tablespoons sun-dried tomato paste*

FOR THE SAUCE
*⅔ cup pitted black olives*
*5 tablespoons capers*
*5 drained anchovy fillets*
*1 red chili, seeded and coarsely chopped*
*4 tablespoons coarsely chopped basil*
*4 tablespoons coarsely chopped parsley*
*⅔ cup olive oil*
*4 ripe tomatoes*
*salt and ground black pepper*
*flat leaf parsley or basil, to garnish*
*Parmesan cheese shavings, to serve*

SERVES 4

1 To make the pasta, sift the flour and salt into a bowl and make a well in the center. Lightly beat the eggs with the tomato paste and pour the mixture into the well.

2 Mix the ingredients together using a round-bladed knife. Turn out onto a work surface and knead for 6–8 minutes until the dough is very smooth and soft, working in a little more flour if it becomes sticky. Wrap in aluminum foil and chill for 30 minutes.

3 To make the sauce, put the olives, capers, anchovies, chili, basil and parsley in a food processor or blender with the oil. Process very briefly until the ingredients are finely chopped. (Alternatively, you can finely chop the ingredients and then mix with the olive oil.)

4 Plunge the tomatoes into boiling water for 30 seconds, then refresh in cold water. Peel away the skins, remove the seeds and dice. Roll out the dough very thinly on a floured surface. Sprinkle with a little flour, then roll up like a jelly roll. Cut across into ½-inch slices.

5 Unroll the pasta and lay out on a clean dish towel for about 10 minutes to dry out.

6 Bring a large saucepan of salted water to the boil. Add the pasta and cook for 2–3 minutes until just tender. Drain immediately and return to the saucepan.

7 Add the olive mixture, tomatoes and salt and black pepper to taste, then toss together gently over moderate heat for about 1 minute until heated through. Garnish with parsley or basil and serve scattered with Parmesan shavings.

# BAKED CHEESE POLENTA WITH TOMATO SAUCE

*Polenta, or cornmeal, is a staple food in Italy. It is cooked like a sort of porridge, and eaten soft, or set, cut into shapes then baked or broiled.*

*1 teaspoon salt*
*2¼ cups quick-cook polenta*
*1 teaspoon paprika*
*½ teaspoon ground nutmeg*
*2 tablespoons olive oil*
*1 large onion, finely chopped*
*2 garlic cloves, crushed*
*2 x 14-ounce cans chopped tomatoes*
*1 tablespoon tomato paste*
*1 teaspoon sugar*
*salt and ground black pepper*
*3 ounces Gruyère cheese, grated*

SERVES 4

1 Preheat the oven to 400°F. Line a baking pan 11 x 7 inches with plastic wrap. Put 4 cups water into a pan and bring to a boil with the salt.

2 Pour in the polenta in a steady stream and cook, stirring continuously, for 5 minutes. Beat in the paprika and nutmeg, then pour into the prepared pan and smooth the surface. Allow to cool.

3 Heat the oil in a pan and cook the onion and garlic until soft. Add the tomatoes, paste and sugar. Season. Simmer for 20 minutes.

4 Turn out the polenta onto a cutting board, and cut into 2-inch squares. Place half the squares in a greased ovenproof dish. Spoon on half the tomato sauce, and sprinkle with half the cheese. Repeat the layers. Bake for about 25 minutes, until golden.

# SPICY CHICKPEA AND EGGPLANT STEW

*This is a Lebanese dish, but similar recipes are found all over the Mediterranean.*

*3 large eggplant, cubed*
*1 cup chickpeas, soaked overnight*
*4 tablespoons olive oil*
*3 garlic cloves, chopped*
*2 large onions, chopped*
*½ teaspoon ground cumin*
*½ teaspoon ground cinnamon*
*2½ teaspoons ground coriander*
*3 x 14-ounce cans chopped tomatoes*
*salt and ground black pepper*
*cooked rice, to serve*

FOR THE GARNISH
*2 tablespoons olive oil*
*1 onion, sliced*
*1 garlic clove, sliced*
*sprigs of coriander*

SERVES 4

1 Place the eggplant in a colander and sprinkle them with salt. Sit the colander in a bowl and leave for 30 minutes, to allow the bitter juices to escape. Rinse with cold water and dry on paper towels.

2 Drain the chickpeas and put in a pan with enough water to cover. Bring to a boil and simmer for 30 minutes, or until tender. Drain.

3 Heat the oil in a large pan. Add the garlic and onion and cook gently, until soft. Add the spices and cook, stirring, for a few seconds. Add the eggplant and stir to coat with the spices and onion. Cook for 5 minutes. Add the tomatoes and chickpeas and season with salt and pepper. Cover and simmer for 20 minutes.

4 To make the garnish, heat the oil in a frying pan and, when very hot, add the sliced onion and garlic. Fry until golden and crisp. Serve the stew with rice, topped with the onion and garlic and garnished with coriander.

# SALADS

*Summer and salads are synonymous, and nowhere is there a wider variety of these flavorful dishes than in the Mediterranean. Salads today range from traditional dishes to new creations: the inspiration for salads is endless. Fruit, such as oranges or grapes, make refreshing additions.*

# ROASTED PEPPERS WITH TOMATOES AND ANCHOVIES

*This is a Sicilian-style salad, using some typical ingredients from the Italian island. The flavor improves if the salad is made and dressed an hour or two before serving.*

*1 red bell pepper*
*1 yellow bell pepper*
*4 sun-dried tomatoes in oil, drained*
*4 ripe plum tomatoes, sliced*
*2 canned anchovies, drained and chopped*
*1 tablespoon capers, drained*
*1 tablespoon pine nuts*
*1 garlic clove, very thinly sliced*

FOR THE DRESSING
*5 tablespoons extra virgin olive oil*
*1 tablespoon balsamic vinegar*
*1 teaspoon lemon juice*
*chopped fresh mixed herbs*
*salt and ground black pepper*

SERVES 4

1 Cut the peppers in half, and remove the seeds and stalks. Cut into quarters and cook, skin side up, under a hot broiler until the skin chars. Transfer to a bowl, and cover with a plate. Allow to cool. Peel the peppers and cut into strips.

2 Thinly slice the sun-dried tomatoes. Arrange the peppers and fresh tomatoes on a serving dish. Scatter on the anchovies, sun-dried tomatoes, capers, pine nuts and garlic.

3 To make the dressing, mix together the olive oil, vinegar, lemon juice and chopped herbs and season with salt and pepper. Pour on the salad just before serving.

# Moroccan Date, Orange and Carrot Salad

*A colorful and unusual salad with exotic ingredients – fresh dates and orange-flower water – combined with crisp greens, carrots, oranges and toasted almonds.*

*1 Bibb lettuce*
*2 carrots, finely grated*
*2 oranges*
*4 ounces fresh dates, stoned and cut into eighths, lengthwise*
*¼ cup toasted whole almonds, chopped*
*2 tablespoons lemon juice*
*1 teaspoon sugar*
*¼ teaspoon salt*
*1 tablespoon orange-flower water*

Serves 4

1 Separate the lettuce leaves and arrange them in the bottom of a salad bowl or on individual serving plates. Place the grated carrot in a mound on top.

2 Peel and segment the oranges and arrange them around the carrot. Pile the dates on top, then sprinkle with the almonds. Mix together the lemon juice, sugar, salt and orange-flower water and sprinkle on the salad. Serve chilled.

# PANZANELLA

*In this lively Italian specialty, a sweet tangy blend of tomato juice, rich olive oil and red wine vinegar is soaked up in a colorful salad of roasted peppers, anchovies and toasted ciabatta.*

*8 ounces ciabatta (about ⅔ loaf)*
*⅔ cup olive oil*
*3 red bell peppers*
*3 yellow bell peppers*
*2-ounce can anchovy fillets*
*1½ pounds ripe plum tomatoes*
*4 garlic cloves, crushed*
*4 tablespoons red wine vinegar*
*2 ounces capers*
*1 cup pitted black olives*
*salt and ground black pepper*
*basil leaves, to garnish*

SERVES 4–6

1. Preheat the oven to 400°F. Cut the ciabatta into ¾-inch chunks and drizzle with ¼ cup of the olive oil. Broil lightly until a pale golden color.

2. Put the peppers on a foil-lined baking sheet and bake for about 45 minutes until the skin begins to char. Remove from the oven, cover with a cloth and allow to cool slightly.

3. Pull the skin off the peppers and cut them into quarters, discarding the stalk ends and seeds. Drain and then coarsely chop the anchovies. Set aside.

4. To make the tomato dressing, peel and halve the tomatoes. Scoop the seeds into a strainer set over a bowl. Using the back of a spoon, press the tomato pulp in the strainer to extract as much juice as possible. Discard the pulp and add the remaining oil, the garlic and vinegar to the juices.

5. Layer the toasted bread, peppers, tomatoes, anchovies, capers and olives in a large salad bowl. Season the tomato dressing with salt and pepper and pour it on the salad. Let stand for about 30 minutes. Serve garnished with plenty of basil leaves.

# RADICCHIO, ARTICHOKE AND WALNUT SALAD

*The distinctive, earthy taste of Jerusalem artichokes makes a lovely contrast to the sharp freshness of radicchio and lemon. Serve warm or cold as an accompaniment to broiled steak or barbecued meats.*

*1 large radicchio or 5 ounces radicchio leaves*
*6 tablespoons walnut pieces*
*3 tablespoons walnut oil*
*1¼ pounds Jerusalem artichokes*
*pared rind and juice of 1 lemon*
*coarse sea salt and ground black pepper*
*flat leaf parsley, to garnish (optional)*

SERVES 4

1. If using a whole radicchio, cut it into 8–10 wedges. Put the wedges or leaves in a flameproof dish. Scatter on the walnuts, then spoon on the oil and season. Broil for 2–3 minutes.

2. Peel the artichokes and cut up any large ones so the pieces are all roughly the same size. Add the artichokes to a pan of boiling salted water with half the lemon juice and cook for 5–7 minutes until tender. Drain. Preheat the broiler to high.

3. Toss the artichokes into the salad with the remaining lemon juice and the pared rind. Season with coarse salt and pepper. Broil until beginning to brown. Serve at once garnished with torn pieces of parsley, if you like.

# WARM FAVA BEAN AND FETA SALAD

*This recipe is loosely based on a typical medley of fresh-tasting Greek salad ingredients – fava beans, tomatoes and feta cheese. It's lovely warm or cold as an appetizer or main course accompaniment.*

*2 pounds fava beans, shelled, or 12 ounces shelled frozen beans*
*4 tablespoons olive oil*
*6 ounces plum tomatoes, halved, or quartered if large*
*4 garlic cloves, crushed*
*4 ounces firm feta cheese, cut into chunks*
*3 tablespoons chopped fresh dill*
*12 black olives*
*salt and ground black pepper*
*chopped fresh dill, to garnish*

SERVES 4–6

1 Cook the fresh or frozen fava beans in boiling, salted water until just tender. Drain and set aside.

2 Meanwhile, heat the oil in a heavy-based frying pan and add the tomatoes and garlic. Cook until the tomatoes are beginning to color.

3 Add the feta to the pan and toss the ingredients together for 1 minute. Mix with the drained beans, dill, olives and salt and pepper. Serve garnished with chopped dill.

# HALLOUMI AND GRAPE SALAD

*In Eastern Europe, firm salty halloumi cheese is often served fried for breakfast or supper. Feta cheese makes a good substitute in this recipe.*

FOR THE DRESSING
*4 tablespoons olive oil*
*1 tablespoon lemon juice*
*½ teaspoon sugar*
*salt and ground black pepper*
*1 tablespoon chopped fresh thyme or dill*

FOR THE SALAD
*5 ounces mixed green salad leaves*
*3 ounces seedless green grapes*
*3 ounces seedless black grapes*
*9 ounces halloumi cheese*
*3 tablespoons olive oil*
*thyme leaves or dill, to garnish*

SERVES 4

1 To make the dressing, mix together the olive oil, lemon juice and sugar. Season. Stir in the thyme or dill and set aside.

2 Toss together the salad greens and the green and black grapes, then transfer to a large serving plate.

3 Thinly slice the cheese. Heat the oil in a large frying pan. Add the cheese and fry briefly until turning golden on the underside. Turn the cheese with a spatula and cook the other side.

4 Arrange the cheese on the salad. Pour on the dressing and garnish with thyme or dill.

# SALAD NICOISE

*Made with good quality ingredients, this Provençal salad makes a simple yet unbeatable summer lunch or supper dish. Serve with country-style bread and chilled white wine.*

FOR THE DRESSING
*6 tablespoons extra virgin olive oil*
*2 garlic cloves, crushed*
*1 tablespoon white wine vinegar*
*salt and ground black pepper*

FOR THE SALAD
*4 ounces green beans, trimmed*
*4 ounces mixed salad greens*
*½ small cucumber, thinly sliced*
*4 ripe tomatoes, quartered*
*7-ounce can tuna in oil, drained*
*2-ounce can anchovies, drained*
*4 eggs, hard-boiled*
*½ bunch radishes, trimmed*
*½ cup small black olives*
*flat leaf parsley, to garnish*

SERVES 4

1 To make the dressing, whisk together the oil, garlic and vinegar and season to taste with salt and pepper.

2 Halve the green beans and cook in a saucepan of boiling water for 2 minutes until only just tender, then drain.

3 Mix the salad greens, cucumber, tomatoes and beans in a large, shallow salad bowl. Flake the tuna. Halve the anchovies lengthwise. Shell and quarter the eggs.

4 Scatter the radishes, tuna, anchovies, eggs and olives on the salad. Pour on the dressing and toss together lightly. Serve garnished with parsley.

# Spanish Asparagus and Orange Salad

*Complicated salad dressings are rarely found in Spain – they simply rely on the wonderful flavor of a good quality olive oil.*

*8 ounces asparagus, trimmed and cut into 2-inch pieces*
*2 large oranges*
*2 well-flavored tomatoes, cut into eighths*
*2 ounces romaine lettuce leaves, shredded*
*2 tablespoons extra virgin olive oil*
*½ teaspoon sherry vinegar*
*salt and ground black pepper*

Serves 4

### Cook's Tip

Bibb lettuce can be used in place of romaine.

1 Cook the asparagus in boiling, salted water for 3–4 minutes, until just tender. Drain and refresh under cold water.

2 Grate the rind from half an orange and reserve. Peel all the oranges and cut into segments. Squeeze out the juice from the membrane and reserve the juice.

3 Put the asparagus, orange segments, tomatoes and lettuce into a salad bowl. Mix together the oil and vinegar and add 1 tablespoon of the reserved orange juice and 1 teaspoon of the rind *(left)*. Season with salt and pepper. Just before serving, pour the dressing on the salad and mix gently to coat.

# Globe Artichokes with Green Beans and Aioli

*Just like the French aïoli, there are many recipes for the Spanish equivalent. This one is exceptionally garlicky, a perfect partner to freshly cooked vegetables.*

For the aioli
*6 large garlic cloves, sliced*
*2 teaspoons white wine vinegar*
*1 cup olive oil*
*salt and ground black pepper*

For the salad
*8 ounces green beans*
*3 small globe artichokes*
*1 tablespoon olive oil*
*pared rind of 1 lemon*
*coarse salt for sprinkling*
*lemon wedges, to garnish*

Serves 4–6

1. To make the aïoli, put the garlic and vinegar in a blender or mini food processor. With the machine switched on, gradually pour in the olive oil until the mixture is thickened and smooth. (Alternatively, crush the garlic to a paste with the vinegar and gradually beat in the oil using a hand whisk.) Season with salt and pepper to taste.

2. To make the salad, cook the beans in boiling water for 1–2 minutes until slightly softened. Drain.

3. Trim the artichoke stalks close to the base. Cook the artichokes in a large pan of salted water for about 30 minutes, or until you can easily pull away a leaf from the base. Drain well.

4. Using a sharp knife, halve the artichokes lengthwise and ease out the choke using a teaspoon.

5. Arrange the artichokes and beans on serving plates and drizzle with the oil. Scatter with the lemon rind and season with coarse salt and a little pepper. Spoon the aïoli into the artichoke hearts and serve warm, garnished with lemon wedges. To eat artichokes, pull the leaves from the base one at a time and use to scoop a little of the sauce. It is only the fleshy end of each leaf that is eaten as well as the base or "heart" of the artichoke.

Cook's Tip

Mediterranean baby artichokes are sometimes available and are perfect for this kind of salad as, unlike the larger ones, they can be eaten whole. Cook them until just tender, then cut in half to serve.

Canned artichoke hearts, thoroughly drained and sliced, can be substituted when fresh ones are not available.

# FAVA BEAN, MUSHROOM AND CHORIZO SALAD

*Fava beans are used in both their fresh and dried forms in various Mediterranean countries. This Spanish salad could be served as either a first course or lunch dish.*

*8 ounces shelled fava beans*
*6 ounces chorizo sausage*
*4 tablespoons extra virgin olive oil*
*8 ounces brown cap mushrooms, sliced*
*handful of fresh chives*
*salt and ground black pepper*

SERVES 4

1 Cook the fava beans in boiling, salted water for about 7–8 minutes. Drain and refresh under cold water.

2 Remove the skin from the sausage and cut it into small chunks. Heat the oil in a frying pan, add the chorizo and cook for 2–3 minutes. Tip the chorizo and oil into the mushrooms and mix well. Allow to cool. Chop half the chives. If the beans are large, peel away the tough outer skins. Stir the beans and snipped chives into the mushroom mixture, and season to taste. Serve at room temperature, garnished with the remaining chives.

# AVOCADO, ORANGE AND ALMOND SALAD

*The Mediterranean is not particularly known for its avocados, but the climate is perfect and they are grown in many parts of the region. This salad has a Spanish influence.*

*2 oranges*
*2 well-flavored tomatoes*
*2 small avocados*
*4 tablespoons extra virgin olive oil*
*2 tablespoons lemon juice*
*1 tablespoon chopped fresh parsley*
*1 small onion, sliced into rings*
*salt and ground black pepper*
*¼ cup flaked almonds and 10–12 black olives, to garnish*

SERVES 4

1 Peel the oranges and cut into thick slices. Plunge the tomatoes into boiling water for 30 seconds, then refresh in cold water. Peel away the skins, cut into quarters, remove the seeds and chop coarsely.

2 Cut the avocados in half, remove the pits and carefully peel away the skin. Cut into chunks.

3 Mix together the olive oil, lemon juice and parsley. Season with salt and pepper. Toss the avocados and tomatoes in half of the dressing.

4 Arrange the sliced oranges on a plate and scatter on the onion rings. Drizzle with the rest of the dressing. Spoon the avocados, tomatoes, almonds and olives on top.

# Fish and Seafood

*Mediterranean fishermen reap a rich harvest of fish and seafood that can be quite unbeatable. Often simply broiled or fried, or used as the basis of a soup or stew, these dishes need little embellishment, except perhaps a crisp salad and a glass or two of light wine!*

# BLACK PASTA WITH SQUID SAUCE

*Tagliatelle flavored with squid ink looks amazing and tastes deliciously of the sea. You'll find it in good Italian delicatessens.*

*7 tablespoons olive oil*
*2 shallots, chopped*
*3 garlic cloves, crushed*
*3 tablespoons chopped fresh parsley*
*1½ pounds cleaned squid, cut into rings and rinsed*
*⅔ cup dry white wine*
*14-ounce can chopped tomatoes*
*½ teaspoon dried chili flakes or powder*
*1 pound squid ink tagliatelle*
*salt and ground black pepper*

SERVES 4

1 Heat the oil in a pan and add the shallots. Cook until pale golden, then add the garlic. When the garlic colors a little, add 2 tablespoons of the parsley, stir, then add the squid and stir again. Cook for 3–4 minutes, then add the wine.

2 Simmer for a few seconds, then add the tomatoes and chili flakes (*right*) and season with salt and pepper. Cover and simmer gently for about 1 hour, until the squid is tender. Add more water if necessary.

3 Cook the pasta in plenty of boiling, salted water, according to the instructions on the packet, or until *al dente*. Drain and return the tagliatelle to the pan. Add the squid sauce and mix well. Sprinkle each serving with the remaining chopped parsley and serve at once.

# SAUTEED MUSSELS WITH GARLIC AND HERBS

*These mussels are served without their shells, in a delicious paprika flavored sauce. Eat them with toothpicks.*

*2 pounds fresh mussels*
*1 lemon slice*
*6 tablespoons olive oil*
*2 shallots, finely chopped*
*1 garlic clove, finely chopped*
*1 tablespoon chopped fresh parsley*
*½ teaspoon sweet paprika*
*¼ teaspoon dried chili flakes*
*parsley sprigs, to garnish*

SERVES 4

1 Scrub the mussels, discarding any damaged ones that do not close when tapped with a knife. Put the mussels in a large pan with 1 cup water and the slice of lemon. Bring to a boil for 3–4 minutes and remove the mussels as they open. Discard any that remain closed. Take the mussels out of the shells and drain them on paper towels.

2 Heat the oil in a sauté pan, add the mussels *(left)* and cook, stirring, for a minute. Remove from the pan. Add the shallots and garlic and cook, covered, over a low heat, for about 5 minutes, until soft. Stir in the parsley, paprika and chili, then add the mussels with any juices. Cook briefly. Remove the pan from the heat, cover and let sit for 1–2 minutes to let the flavors mingle. Serve, garnished with parsley.

# Grilled Jumbo Shrimp with Romesco Sauce

*This sauce, from the Catalan region of Spain, is served with fish and seafood. Its main ingredients are sweet bell pepper, tomatoes, garlic and almonds.*

*24 raw jumbo shrimp*
*2–3 tablespoons olive oil*
*flat leaf parsley, to garnish*
*lemon wedges, to serve*

For the sauce
*2 well-flavored tomatoes*
*4 tablespoons olive oil*
*1 onion, chopped*
*4 garlic cloves, chopped*
*1 canned pimiento, chopped*
*½ teaspoon dried chili flakes or powder*
*5 tablespoons fish stock*
*2 tablespoons white wine*
*10 blanched almonds*
*1 tablespoon red wine vinegar*
*salt*

Serves 4

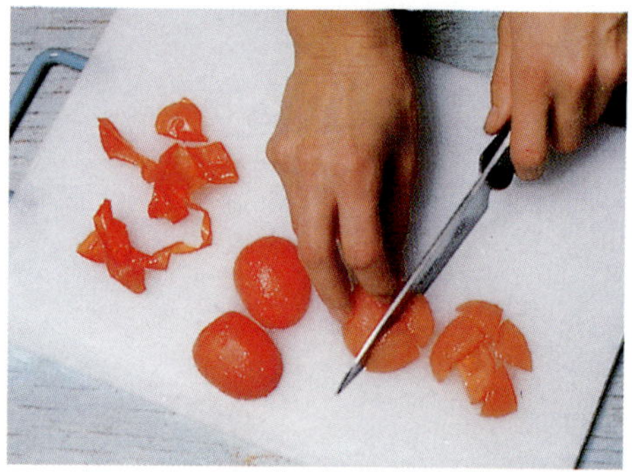

1 To make the sauce, immerse the tomatoes in boiling water for about 30 seconds, then refresh them under cold water. Peel away the skins and coarsely chop the flesh.

2 Heat 2 tablespoons of the oil in a pan, add the onion and 3 of the garlic cloves and cook until soft. Add the pimiento, tomatoes, chili, fish stock and wine, then cover and simmer for 30 minutes.

3 Toast the almonds under the broiler until golden. Transfer to a blender or food processor and grind coarsely. Add the remaining 2 tablespoons of oil, the vinegar and the last garlic clove and process until evenly combined. Add the tomato and pimiento sauce and process until smooth. Season with salt.

4 Remove the heads from the shrimp leaving them otherwise unshelled and, with a sharp knife, slit each one down the back and remove the dark vein. Rinse and pat dry on paper towels. Preheat the broiler. Toss the shrimp in olive oil, then spread out in the broiler pan. Broil for about 2–3 minutes on each side, until pink. Arrange on a serving platter with the lemon wedges, and the sauce in a small bowl. Serve immediately, garnished with parsley.

# Brodetto

*The different regions of Italy have their own variations of this dish, but all require a good fish stock. Make sure you buy some of the fish whole so you can simply simmer them, remove the cooked flesh and strain the deliciously flavored juices to make the stock.*

*2-pound mixture of fish fillets or steaks, such as monkfish, cod, haddock, halibut or hake*
*2-pound mixture of conger eel, red or gray mullet, snapper or small white fish*
*1 onion, halved*
*1 celery stalk, coarsely chopped*
*8 ounces squid*
*8 ounces fresh mussels*
*1½ pounds ripe tomatoes*
*4 tablespoons olive oil*
*1 large onion, thinly sliced*
*3 garlic cloves, crushed*
*1 teaspoon saffron strands*
*⅔ cup dry white wine*
*6 tablespoons chopped fresh parsley*
*salt and ground black pepper*
*croûtons, to serve*

Serves 4–5

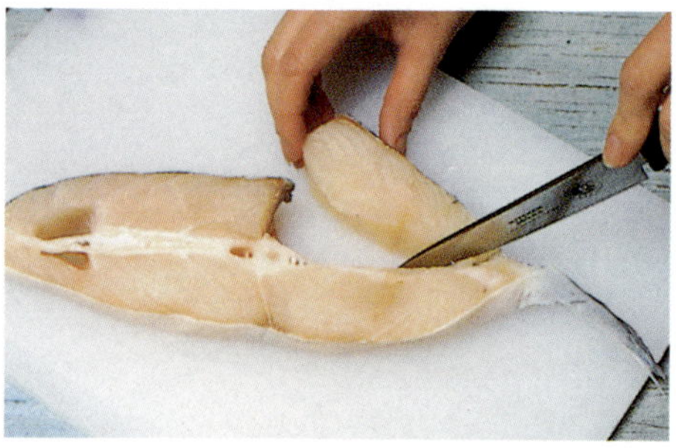

1 Remove any skin and bones from the fish fillets or steaks, cut the fish into large pieces and reserve. Place the bones in a pan with all the remaining fish.

2 Add the halved onion and the celery and just cover with water. Bring almost to a boil, then reduce the heat and simmer gently for about 30 minutes. Lift out the fish and remove the flesh from the bones. Reserve the stock.

3 To prepare the squid, twist the head and tentacles away from the body. Cut the head from the tentacles. Discard the body contents and peel away the mottled skin. Wash the tentacles and bodies and dry on paper towels.

### Cook's Tip

To make the croûtons, cut thin slices from a long thin stick of bread and shallow fry in a little butter until golden.

4 Scrub the mussels, discarding any that are damaged or open ones that do not close when tapped.

5 Plunge the tomatoes into boiling water for 30 seconds, then refresh in cold water. Peel away the skins and chop coarsely.

6 Heat the oil in a large saucepan or sauté pan. Add the sliced onion and the garlic and fry gently for 3 minutes. Add the squid and the uncooked white fish, which you reserved earlier, and fry quickly on all sides. Drain.

7 Add 2 cups strained reserved fish stock, the saffron and tomatoes to the pan. Pour in the wine. Bring to a boil, then reduce the heat and simmer for about 5 minutes. Add the mussels, cover, and cook for 3–4 minutes until the mussels have opened. Discard any that remain closed.

8 Season the sauce with salt and pepper and put all the fish in the pan. Cook gently for 5 minutes. Scatter with the parsley and serve with the croûtons.

# SARDINE GRATIN

*In Sicily and other countries in the Western Mediterranean, sardines are filled with a robust stuffing, flavorful enough to compete with the rich oiliness of the fish itself.*

*1 tablespoon light olive oil*
*½ small onion, finely chopped*
*2 garlic cloves, crushed*
*6 tablespoons blanched almonds, chopped*
*2 tablespoons golden raisins, coarsely chopped*
*10 pitted black olives*
*2 tablespoons capers, coarsely chopped*
*2 tablespoons coarsely chopped fresh parsley*
*1 cup bread crumbs*
*16 large sardines, scaled and gutted*
*⅓ cup grated Parmesan cheese*
*salt and ground black pepper*
*flat leaf parsley, to garnish*

SERVES 4

1 Preheat the oven to 400°F. Lightly oil a large shallow ovenproof dish.

2 Heat the oil in a frying pan and fry the onion and garlic gently for 3 minutes. Stir in the almonds, raisins, olives, capers, parsley and ¼ cup of the bread crumbs. Season lightly with salt and pepper.

*ABOVE: Brodetto (top) and Sardine Gratin (bottom)*

3 Make 2–3 diagonal cuts on each side of the sardines. Pack the stuffing into the cavities and lay the sardines in the prepared dish.

4 Mix the remaining bread crumbs with the cheese and scatter on the fish. Bake for about 20 minutes until the fish is cooked through. Test by piercing one sardine through the thickest part with a knife. Garnish with parsley and serve immediately with a leafy salad.

# Hake and Clams with Salsa Verde

*Hake is one of the most popular fish in Spain and here it is cooked in a sauce flavored with parsley, lemon juice and garlic.*

*4 hake steaks, about ¾-inch thick*
*½ cup flour for dusting, plus*
*2 tablespoons*
*4 tablespoons olive oil*
*1 tablespoon lemon juice*
*1 small onion, finely chopped*
*4 garlic cloves, crushed*
*⅔ cup fish stock*
*⅔ cup white wine*
*6 tablespoons chopped fresh parsley*
*3 ounces frozen petits pois*
*16 fresh clams*
*salt and ground black pepper*

Serves 4

1 Preheat the oven to 350°F. Season the fish with salt and pepper, then dust both sides with flour. Heat 2 tablespoons of the oil in a large sauté pan, add the fish and fry for about 1 minute on each side. Transfer to an ovenproof dish and sprinkle with lemon juice.

2 Clean the pan, then heat the remaining oil. Add the onion and garlic and cook until soft. Stir in 2 tablespoons flour and cook for about 1 minute. Gradually add the stock and wine, stirring until thickened and smooth. Add 5 tablespoons of the parsley and the petits pois and season with salt and pepper.

3 Pour the sauce over the fish, and bake in the oven for 15–20 minutes, adding the clams to the dish 3–4 minutes before the end of the cooking time. Discard any clams that do not open, then sprinkle with the remaining parsley before serving.

# Sicilian Spaghetti with Sardines

*A traditional dish from Sicily, with ingredients that are common to many parts of the Mediterranean.*

*12 fresh sardines, cleaned and boned*
*1 cup olive oil*
*1 onion, chopped*
*¼ cup dill sprigs*
*½ cup pine nuts*
*2 tablespoons raisins, soaked in water*
*½ cup fresh bread crumbs*
*1 pound spaghetti*
*flour for dusting*
*salt*

Serves 4

1 Wash the sardines and pat dry on paper towels. Open them out flat, then cut in half lengthwise.

2 Heat 2 tablespoons of the oil in a pan, add the onion and fry until golden. Add the dill and cook gently for a minute or two. Add the pine nuts and raisins and season with salt. Dry-fry the bread crumbs in a frying pan until golden. Set aside.

3 Cook the spaghetti in boiling, salted water according to the instructions on the package, until *al dente*. Heat the remaining oil in a pan. Dust the sardines with flour and fry in the hot oil for 2–3 minutes. Drain on paper towels.

4 Drain the spaghetti and return to the pan. Add the onion mixture and toss well. Transfer the spaghetti mixture to a serving platter and arrange the fried sardines on top. Sprinkle with the toasted bread crumbs and serve immediately.

# SEAFOOD RISOTTO

*Risotto is one of Italy's most popular rice dishes and it is made with everything from pumpkin to squid ink. On the Mediterranean shores, seafood is the most obvious addition.*

*4 tablespoons sunflower oil*
*1 onion, chopped*
*2 garlic cloves, crushed*
*generous 1 cup arborio rice*
*7 tablespoons white wine*
*6¼ cups hot fish stock*
*12 ounces mixed seafood, such as raw shrimp, mussels, squid rings or clams*
*grated rind of ½ lemon*
*2 tablespoons tomato paste*
*1 tablespoon chopped fresh parsley*
*salt and ground black pepper*

SERVES 4

1 Heat the oil in a heavy-based pan, add the onion and garlic and cook until soft. Add the rice and stir to coat the grains with oil. Add the wine and cook over moderate heat, stirring, for a few minutes until absorbed.

2 Add ⅔ cup of the hot fish stock and cook, stirring constantly, until the liquid is absorbed by the rice. Continue stirring and adding stock in ⅔ cup quantities, until half of the stock is left. This should take about 10 minutes.

3 Stir in the seafood and cook for 2–3 minutes. Add the remaining stock as before, until the rice is cooked. It should be quite creamy and the grains *al dente*.

4 Stir in the lemon rind, tomato paste and parsley. Season with salt and pepper and serve warm.

# ITALIAN SHRIMP SKEWERS

*Simple and delicious mouthfuls from the Amalfi Coast.*

*2 pounds raw shrimp, peeled*
*4 tablespoons olive oil*
*3 tablespoons vegetable oil*
*1¼ cups very fine dry bread crumbs*
*1 garlic clove, crushed*
*1 tablespoon chopped fresh parsley*
*salt and ground black pepper*
*lemon wedges, to serve*

SERVES 4

1 Slit the shrimp down their backs and remove the dark vein. Rinse in cold water and pat dry.

2 Put the olive oil and vegetable oil in a large bowl and add the shrimp, mixing them to coat evenly. Add the bread crumbs, garlic and parsley and season with salt and pepper. Toss the shrimp thoroughly, to give them an even coating of bread crumbs. Cover and let marinate for at least 1 hour.

3 Thread the shrimp onto four metal or wooden skewers, curling them up as you do so, so that the tail is skewered in the middle.

4 Preheat the broiler. Place the skewers in the broiler pan and cook for about 2 minutes on each side, until the bread crumbs are golden. Serve with lemon wedges.

# ZARZUELA

*Zarzuela means "light opera" or "musical comedy" in Spanish and the classic fish stew of the same name should be as lively and colorful as the zarzuela itself. This feast of fish includes lobster and other shellfish, but you can modify the ingredients to suit the occasion and availability.*

*1 cooked lobster*
*24 fresh mussels or clams*
*1 large monkfish tail*
*8 ounces squid rings*
*1 tablespoon flour*
*6 tablespoons olive oil*
*12 large raw shrimp*
*1 pound ripe tomatoes*
*2 large mild onions, chopped*
*4 garlic cloves, crushed*
*2 tablespoons brandy*
*2 bay leaves*
*1 teaspoon paprika*
*1 red chili, seeded and chopped*
*1¼ cups fish stock*
*2 tablespoons ground almonds*
*2 tablespoons chopped fresh parsley*
*salt and ground black pepper*

SERVES 6

1 Using a large knife, cut the lobster in half lengthwise. Remove the dark intestine that runs down the length of the tail. Crack the claws using a hammer.

2 Scrub the mussels, discarding any that are damaged or open ones that do not close when tapped with a knife. Cut the monkfish fillets away from the central cartilage and cut each fillet into three.

3 Toss the monkfish and squid in seasoned flour. Heat the oil in a large frying pan. Add the monkfish and squid and fry quickly; remove from the pan. Fry the shrimp on both sides, then remove from the pan.

4 Plunge the tomatoes into boiling water for 30 seconds, then refresh in cold water. Peel away the skins and chop coarsely.

5 Add the onions and two-thirds of the garlic to the frying pan and fry, stirring thoroughly for about 3 minutes. Add the brandy and ignite. When the flames die down, add the tomatoes, bay leaves, paprika, chili and stock.

6 Bring to a boil, reduce the heat and simmer gently for 5 minutes. Add the mussels or clams, cover and cook for 3–4 minutes, until the shells have opened.

7 Remove the mussels or clams from the sauce and discard any that remain closed.

8 Arrange all the fish, including the lobster, in a large flameproof serving dish. Blend the ground almonds to a paste with the remaining garlic and parsley and stir into the sauce. Season with salt and pepper.

9 Pour the sauce on the fish and lobster and cook gently for about 5 minutes until hot. Serve immediately with a green salad and plenty of warmed bread.

# MEAT AND POULTRY

*The Mediterranean style of cooking makes the most of young lamb and pork, while lighter meats, such as poultry and game, play key roles in regional cuisines right across the Mediterranean. The addition of fruit or vegetables creates sensational flavor combinations.*

# LAMB WITH RED BELL PEPPERS AND RIOJA

*Plenty of garlic, peppers, herbs and red wine give this lamb stew a lovely rich flavor. Slice through the pepper stalks, rather than removing them, as this makes it look extra special.*

*2 pounds lean lamb fillet*
*1 tablespoon flour*
*4 tablespoons olive oil*
*2 red skinned onions, sliced*
*4 garlic cloves, sliced*
*2 teaspoons paprika*
*¼ teaspoon ground cloves*
*1⅔ cups red Rioja wine*
*⅔ cup lamb stock*
*2 bay leaves*
*2 thyme sprigs*
*3 red bell peppers, halved and seeded*
*salt and ground black pepper*
*bay leaves and thyme sprigs, to garnish*
*green beans and saffron rice or boiled potatoes, to serve*

SERVES 4

1 Preheat the oven to 325°F. Cut the lamb into chunks. Season the flour, add the lamb and toss lightly to coat.

2 Heat the oil in a frying pan and fry the lamb, stirring, until browned. Transfer to an ovenproof dish. Lightly fry the onions in the pan with the garlic, paprika and cloves.

3 Add the Rioja, stock, bay leaves and thyme and bring to a boil, stirring. Pour the contents of the pan onto the meat. Cover with a lid and bake for 30 minutes.

4 Remove the dish from the oven. Stir the red bell peppers into the stew and season lightly with salt and pepper. Bake for another 30 minutes until the meat is tender. Garnish the stew with bay leaves and sprigs of thyme and serve with green beans and saffron rice or boiled potatoes.

### VARIATION

Use any lean cubed pork instead of the lamb and a white Rioja wine instead of the red. A mixture of red, yellow and orange bell peppers looks very effective.

# PORK WITH MARSALA WINE AND JUNIPER

*Although most frequently used in desserts, Sicilian marsala gives savory dishes a rich, fruity and alcoholic tang. Use good quality butcher's pork which won't be drowned by the flavor of the sauce.*

*1 ounce dried cèpes or porcini mushrooms*
*4 pork scallops*
*2 teaspoons balsamic vinegar*
*8 garlic cloves*
*1 tablespoon butter*
*3 tablespoons marsala wine*
*several rosemary sprigs*
*10 juniper berries, crushed*
*salt and ground black pepper*
*noodles and green vegetables, to serve*

SERVES 4

1 Put the dried mushrooms in a bowl and just cover with hot water. Let stand.

2 Brush the pork with 1 teaspoon of the vinegar and season with salt and pepper. Put the garlic cloves in a small pan of boiling water and cook for 10 minutes until soft. Drain and set aside.

3 Melt the butter in a large frying pan. Add the pork and fry quickly until browned on the underside. Turn the meat over and cook for another minute.

4 Add the marsala, rosemary, mushrooms, 4 tablespoons of the mushroom juices, the garlic cloves, juniper and remaining vinegar.

5 Simmer gently for about 3 minutes until the pork is cooked through. Season lightly and serve hot with noodles and green vegetables.

# CHICKEN THIGHS WITH LEMON AND GARLIC

*This recipe uses classic flavorings for chicken. Versions of it can be found in Spain and Italy. This particular recipe, however, is of French origin.*

*2½ cups chicken stock*
*20 large garlic cloves*
*2 tablespoons butter*
*1 tablespoon olive oil*
*8 chicken thighs*
*1 lemon, peeled, pith removed and sliced thinly*
*2 tablespoons flour*
*⅔ cup dry white wine*
*salt and ground black pepper*
*chopped fresh parsley or basil, to garnish*
*new potatoes or rice, to serve*

SERVES 4

1 Put the stock into a pan and bring to a boil. Add the garlic cloves, cover and simmer gently for 40 minutes. Heat the butter and oil in a sauté or frying pan, add the chicken thighs and cook gently on all sides until golden. Transfer them to an ovenproof dish. Preheat the oven to 375°F.

2 Strain the stock and reserve it. Distribute the garlic and lemon slices among the chicken pieces. Add the flour to the fat in the pan in which the chicken was browned, and cook, stirring, for 1 minute. Add the wine, stirring constantly and scraping the bottom of the pan, then add the stock. Cook, stirring, until the sauce has thickened and is smooth. Season with salt and pepper.

3 Pour the sauce on the chicken, cover, and cook in the oven for 40–45 minutes. If a thicker sauce is required, lift out the chicken pieces, and reduce the sauce by boiling rapidly, until it reaches the desired consistency. Scatter on the chopped parsley or basil and serve with boiled new potatoes or rice.

# POLPETTES WITH MOZZARELLA AND TOMATO

*These Italian meatballs are made with beef and topped with mozzarella cheese and tomato.*

*½ slice white bread, crusts removed*
*3 tablespoons milk*
*1½ pounds ground beef*
*1 egg, beaten*
*⅔ cup dry bread crumbs*
*vegetable oil for frying*
*2 beefsteak or other large tomatoes, sliced*
*1 tablespoon chopped fresh oregano*
*1 mozzarella cheese, cut into 6 slices*
*6 drained canned anchovies, cut in half lengthwise*
*salt and ground black pepper*

SERVES 6

1 Preheat the oven to 400°F. Put the bread and milk into a small saucepan and heat very gently over low heat, until the bread absorbs all the milk. Mash it to a pulp and allow to cool.

2 Put the beef into a bowl with the bread mixture and the egg and season with salt and pepper. Mix well, then shape the mixture into six patties. Sprinkle the bread crumbs on to a plate and dredge the patties, coating them thoroughly.

3 Heat about ¼-inch oil in a large frying pan. Add the patties and fry for 2 minutes on each side, until brown. Transfer to a greased ovenproof dish, in a single layer.

4 Lay a slice of tomato on top of each patty, sprinkle with oregano and season with salt and pepper. Place the mozzarella slices on top. Arrange two strips of anchovy, placed in a cross on top of each slice of mozzarella.

5 Bake for 10–15 minutes, until the mozzarella has melted. Serve hot, straight from the dish.

# Olive Oil Roasted Chicken with Mediterranean Vegetables

*This is a delicious French alternative to a traditional roast chicken. Use a corn-fed or free-range bird, if available. This recipe also works well with guinea fowl.*

*4½-pound roasting chicken*
*⅔ cup extra virgin olive oil*
*½ lemon*
*few sprigs of fresh thyme*
*1 pound small new potatoes*
*1 eggplant, cut into 1-inch cubes*
*1 red bell pepper, seeded and quartered*
*1 fennel bulb, trimmed and quartered*
*8 large garlic cloves, unpeeled*
*coarse salt and ground black pepper*

SERVES 4

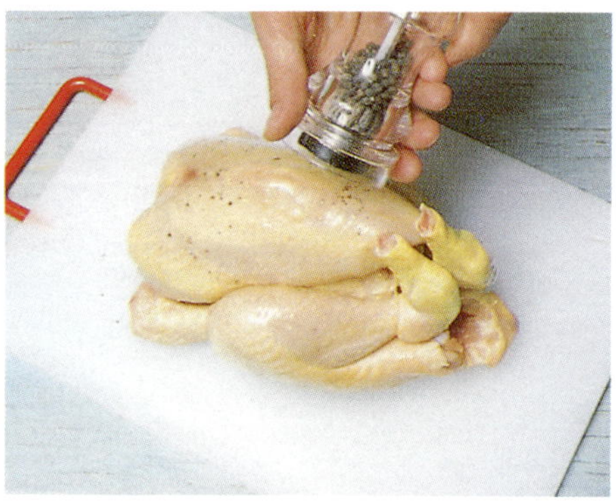

1 Preheat the oven to 400°F. Rub the chicken all over with olive oil and season with pepper. Place the lemon half inside the bird, with a sprig or two of thyme. Put the chicken breast side down in a large roasting pan. Roast for about 30 minutes.

2 Remove the chicken from the oven and season with salt. Turn the chicken right side up, and baste with the drippings from the pan. Surround the bird with the potatoes, roll them in the pan drippings, and return the roasting pan to the oven, to continue roasting.

3 After 30 minutes, add the eggplant, red bell pepper, fennel and garlic cloves to the pan. Drizzle with the remaining oil, and season with salt and pepper. Add any remaining thyme to the vegetables. Return to the oven, and cook for 30–50 minutes more, basting and turning the vegetables occasionally.

4 To find out if the chicken is cooked, push the tip of a sharp knife between the thigh and breast. If the juices run clear, it is done. The vegetables should be tender and just beginning to brown. Serve the chicken and vegetables from the pan, or transfer the vegetables to a serving dish, cut up the chicken and place it on top. Serve the skimmed juices in a gravy boat.

# PIGEON BREASTS WITH PANCETTA

*Mild succulent pigeon breasts are easy to cook and make an impressive main course for a special dinner. Serve this Italian-style dish with polenta and some simple green vegetables.*

*4 whole pigeons*
*2 large onions*
*2 carrots, coarsely chopped*
*1 celery stalk, trimmed and coarsely chopped*
*1 ounce dried porcini mushrooms*
*2 ounces pancetta*
*2 tablespoons butter*
*2 tablespoons olive oil*
*2 garlic cloves, crushed*
*⅔ cup red wine*
*salt and ground black pepper*
*flat leaf parsley, to garnish*
*cooked oyster mushrooms, to serve*

SERVES 4

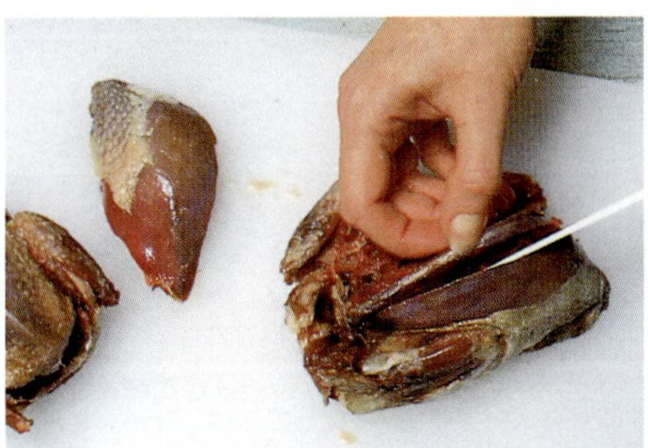

1 To prepare a pigeon, cut down the length of the bird, just to one side of the breastbone. Gradually scrape away the meat from the breastbone until the breast comes away completely. Do the same on the other side, then repeat with the remaining pigeons.

2 Put the pigeon carcasses in a large saucepan. Halve one of the onions, leaving the skin on. Add to the pan with the carrots and celery and just cover with water. Bring to a boil, reduce the heat and simmer very gently, uncovered, for about 1½ hours to make a dark, rich stock. Let cool slightly, then strain into a bowl.

3 Cover the porcini mushrooms with ⅔ cup hot water and allow to soak for at least 30 minutes. Chop the pancetta.

4 Peel and finely chop the remaining onion. Melt half the butter with the oil in a large frying pan. Add the onion and pancetta and fry very gently for 3 minutes. Add the pigeon breasts, skin sides down and fry for 2 minutes until browned. Turn over and fry for another 2 minutes.

5 Add the mushrooms, with the soaking liquid, garlic, wine and 1 cup of the stock. Bring just to a boil, then reduce the heat and simmer gently for 5 minutes until the pigeon breasts are tender, but still a little pink in the center.

6 Lift out the pigeon breasts and keep them hot. Return the sauce to a boil and boil rapidly to reduce slightly. Gradually whisk in all the remaining butter and season with salt and pepper to taste.

7 Transfer the pigeon breasts to warmed serving plates and pour on the sauce. Serve at once, garnished with sprigs of parsley and accompanied by oyster mushrooms.

### COOK'S TIP

If buying pigeons from a butcher, order them in advance and ask him to remove the breasts for you. You can also cut off the legs and fry these with the breasts, although there is little meat on them and you might prefer to let them flavor the stock.

# Breads, Pastries and Desserts

*Bread, a staple food all over the Mediterranean, comes in a remarkable variety of flavors and textures, while sumptuous pastries and desserts provide a fabulous finale to any meal.*

# SUN-DRIED TOMATO BREAD

*In the south of Italy, tomatoes are often dried off in the hot sun. They are then preserved in oil, or hung up in strings in the kitchen, to use in the winter. This recipe uses the former.*

*6 cups strong flour*
*2 teaspoons salt*
*2 tablespoons sugar*
*1 ounce fresh yeast*
*1⅔–2 cups warm milk*
*1 tablespoon tomato paste*
*5 tablespoons oil from the jar of sun-dried tomatoes*
*5 tablespoons extra virgin olive oil*
*¾ cup drained sun-dried tomatoes, chopped*
*1 large onion, chopped*

MAKES 4 SMALL LOAVES

1 Sift the flour, salt and sugar into a bowl, and make a well in the center. Crumble the yeast, mix with ⅔ cup of the warm milk and add to the flour.

COOK'S TIP
Use a pair of sharp kitchen scissors to cut up the sun-dried tomatoes.

2 Mix the tomato paste into the remaining milk, until evenly blended, then add to the flour with the tomato oil and olive oil.

3 Gradually mix the flour into the liquid ingredients, until you have a dough. Turn out onto a floured surface, and knead for about 10 minutes, until smooth and elastic. Return to the clean bowl, cover with a cloth, and let rise in a warm place for about 2 hours.

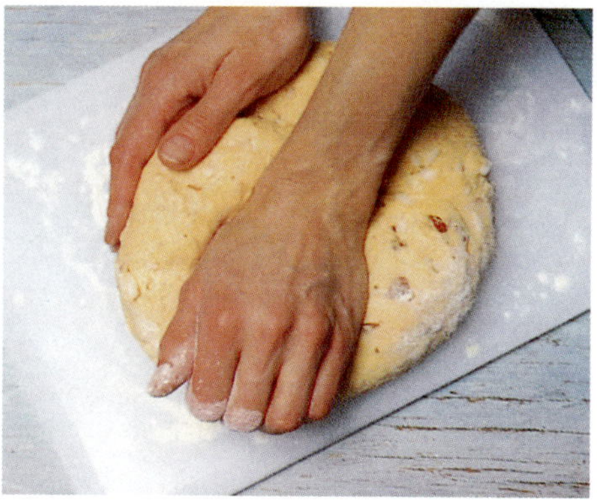

4 Punch down, and add the tomatoes and onion. Knead until evenly distributed through the dough. Shape into four loaves and place on a greased baking sheet. Cover with a dish towel and allow to rise again for about 45 minutes.

5 Preheat the oven to 375°F. Bake the bread for 45 minutes, or until the loaves sound hollow when you tap them underneath with your fingers. Allow to cool on a wire rack. Eat warm, or toasted with grated mozzarella cheese sprinkled on top.

# OLIVE BREAD

*Olive breads are popular all over the Mediterranean. For this Greek recipe use rich oily olives or those marinated in herbs rather than canned ones.*

*2 red onions, thinly sliced*
*2 tablespoons olive oil*
*1⅓ cups pitted black or green olives*
*7 cups strong flour*
*1½ teaspoons salt*
*4 teaspoons fast-rising dried yeast*
*3 tablespoons each coarsely chopped parsley, coriander or mint*

MAKES TWO 1½-POUND LOAVES

1. Fry the onions in the oil until soft. Coarsely chop the olives.

2. Put the flour, salt, yeast and parsley, coriander or mint in a large bowl with the olives and fried onions and pour in 2 cups hand-hot water.

### VARIATION

Shape the dough into 16 small rolls. Slash the tops as above and reduce the cooking time to 25 minutes.

3. Mix to a dough using a round-bladed knife, adding a little more water if the mixture feels dry.

4. Turn out onto a lightly floured surface and knead for about 10 minutes. Put in a clean bowl, cover with plastic wrap and leave in a warm place until doubled in bulk.

5. Preheat the oven to 425°F. Lightly grease two baking sheets. Turn the dough onto a floured surface and cut in half. Shape into two loaves and place on the baking sheets. Cover loosely with lightly oiled plastic wrap and let rise until doubled in size.

6. Slash the tops of the loaves with a knife, then bake for about 40 minutes or until the loaves sound hollow when tapped on the bottom. Transfer to a wire rack to cool.

# FOCACCIA

*This is a flattish bread, originating from Genoa in Italy, made with flour, olive oil and salt. There are many variations, from many regions, including stuffed varieties, and versions topped with onions, olives or herbs.*

*1 ounce fresh yeast*
*3½ cups strong flour*
*2 teaspoons salt*
*5 tablespoons olive oil*
*2 teaspoons coarse sea salt*

MAKES 1 ROUND 10-INCH LOAF

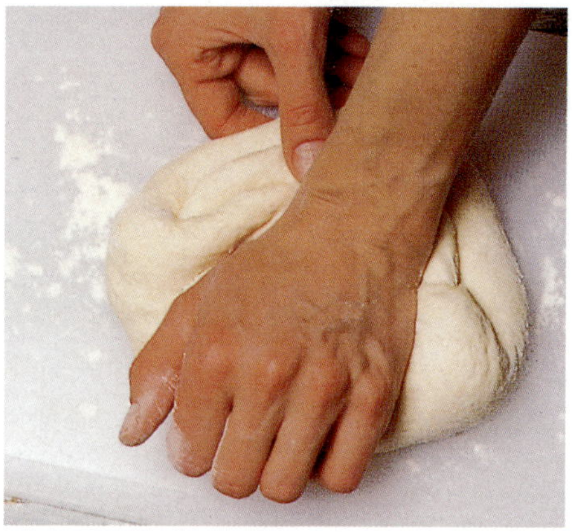

1 Dissolve the yeast in ½ cup warm water. Allow to stand for 10 minutes. Sift the flour into a large bowl, make a well in the center, and add the yeast, salt and 2 tablespoons oil. Mix in the flour and add more water to make a dough.

2 Turn out onto a floured surface and knead the dough for about 10 minutes, until smooth and elastic. Return to the bowl, cover with a cloth, and allow to rise in a warm place for 2–2½ hours until the dough has doubled in bulk.

3 Punch down the dough and knead again for a few minutes. Press into an oiled 10-inch tart pan, and cover with a damp cloth. Let rise for 30 minutes.

4 Preheat the oven to 400°F. Poke the dough all over with your fingers, to make little dimples in the surface. Pour the remaining oil on the dough, using a pastry brush to take it to the edges. Sprinkle with the salt.

5 Bake for 20–25 minutes, until the bread is pale gold. Carefully remove from the pan and let cool on a rack. The bread is best eaten on the same day, but it also freezes very well.

# FRESH FIGS WITH HONEY AND WINE

*Any variety of figs can be used in this recipe, their ripeness determining the cooking time. Choose ones that are plump and firm, and use quickly as they don't store well.*

*1⅞ cups dry white wine*
*⅓ cup honey*
*¼ cup sugar*
*1 small orange*
*8 whole cloves*
*1 pound fresh figs*
*1 cinnamon stick*
*mint sprigs, or bay leaves, to decorate*

FOR THE CREAM
*1¼ cups heavy cream*
*1 vanilla pod*
*1 teaspoon sugar*

SERVES 6

1 Put the wine, honey and sugar in a heavy-based saucepan and heat gently until the sugar dissolves.

2 Stud the orange with the cloves and add to the syrup with the figs and cinnamon. Cover and simmer very gently for 5–10 minutes until the figs are softened. Transfer to a serving dish and allow to cool.

3 Put ⅔ cup of the cream in a small saucepan with the vanilla pod. Bring almost to a boil, then let cool and infuse for 30 minutes. Remove the vanilla pod and mix with the remaining cream and sugar in a bowl. Whip lightly. Transfer to a serving dish. Decorate the figs, then serve with the cream.

# ICED ORANGES

*These little sherbets served in the fruit shell were originally sold in the beach cafés in the south of France. They are pretty and easy to eat – a good picnic treat to store in the cooler.*

*⅔ cup sugar*
*juice of 1 lemon*
*14 medium oranges*
*8 fresh bay leaves, to decorate*

SERVES 8

1 Put the sugar in a heavy-based pan. Add half the lemon juice, and ½ cup water. Cook over low heat until the sugar has dissolved completely. Bring to a boil, and boil for 2–3 minutes, until the syrup is clear. Allow to cool.

2 Slice the tops off eight of the oranges, to make "hats." Scoop out the flesh of the oranges, and reserve. Put the empty orange shells and "hats" on a tray and place in the freezer until needed.

3 Grate the rind of the remaining oranges and add to the syrup. Squeeze the juice from the oranges, and from the reserved flesh. There should be 3 cups. Squeeze another orange or add bought orange juice, if necessary.

4 Stir the orange juice and remaining lemon juice, with 6 tablespoons water into the syrup. Taste, adding more lemon juice or sugar, as desired. Pour the mixture into a shallow freezer container and freeze for 3 hours.

5 Turn the mixture into a bowl, and whisk to break down the ice crystals. Freeze for 4 hours more, until firm, but not solid.

6 Pack the mixture into the orange shells, mounding it up, and set the "hats" on top. Freeze until ready to serve. Just before serving, push a skewer into the tops of the "hats" and push in a bay leaf.

COOK'S TIP
Use crumpled paper towels to keep the shells upright.

# WALNUT AND RICOTTA CAKE

*Soft, tangy ricotta cheese is widely used in Italian desserts. Here, it is included along with walnuts and orange to flavor a whisked egg spongecake. Don't worry if it sinks slightly after baking – this gives it an authentic appearance.*

*1 cup walnut pieces*
*⅔ cup sweet butter, softened*
*⅔ cup sugar*
*5 eggs, separated*
*finely grated rind of 1 orange*
*⅔ cup ricotta cheese*
*6 tablespoons flour*

TO FINISH
*4 tablespoons apricot jam*
*2 tablespoons brandy*
*2 ounces unsweetened or semisweet chocolate, coarsely grated*

MAKES 10 SLICES

1 Preheat the oven to 375°F. Grease and line the base of a deep 9-inch round, loose-based cake pan. Coarsely chop and lightly toast the walnuts.

2 Cream together the butter and ½ cup of the sugar until light and fluffy. Add the egg yolks, orange rind, ricotta cheese, flour and walnuts and mix together.

3 Whisk the egg whites in a large bowl until stiff. Gradually whisk in the remaining sugar. Using a large metal spoon, fold a quarter of the whisked whites into the ricotta mixture. Carefully fold in the rest of the whisked whites.

4 Turn the mixture into the prepared pan and level the surface. Bake for about 30 minutes until risen and firm. Allow the cake to cool in the tin.

5 Transfer the cake to a serving plate. Heat the apricot jam in a small saucepan with 1 tablespoon water. Strain and stir in the brandy. Use to coat the top and sides of the cake. Scatter the cake generously with grated chocolate.

VARIATION
Use toasted and chopped almonds in place of the walnuts.

# BISCOTTI

*These lovely Italian cookies are part-baked, sliced to reveal a feast of mixed nuts and then baked again until crisp and golden. Traditionally they're served dipped in Vin Santo, a sweet dessert wine - perfect for rounding off a Mediterranean meal.*

*¼ cup sweet butter, softened*
*½ cup sugar*
*1½ cups self-rising flour*
*¼ teaspoon salt*
*2 teaspoons baking powder*
*1 teaspoon ground coriander*
*finely grated rind of 1 lemon*
*½ cup polenta*
*1 egg, lightly beaten*
*2 teaspoons brandy or orange-flavored liqueur*
*½ cup unblanched almonds*
*½ cup pistachio nuts*

MAKES 24

1 Preheat the oven to 325°F. Lightly grease a baking sheet. Cream together the butter and sugar.

2 Sift all the flour, salt, baking powder and coriander into the bowl. Add the lemon rind, polenta, egg and brandy or liqueur and mix together to make a soft dough.

3 Stir in the nuts until evenly combined. Halve the mixture. Shape each half into a flat sausage about 9 inches long and 2½ inches wide. Bake for about 30 minutes until risen and just firm. Remove from oven.

4 When cool, cut each sausage diagonally into 12 thin slices. Return to the baking sheet and cook for another 10 minutes until crisp.

5 Transfer to a wire rack to cool completely. Store in an airtight jar for up to 1 week.

COOK'S TIP

Use a sharp, serrated knife to slice the cooled cookies, otherwise they will crumble.

# DATE AND ALMOND TART

*Fresh dates make an unusual but delicious filling for a tart. The influences here are French and Middle Eastern – a true Mediterranean fusion!*

FOR THE PASTRY
*1½ cups flour*
*6 tablespoons butter*
*1 egg*

FOR THE FILLING
*scant ½ cup butter*
*7 tablespoons sugar*
*1 egg, beaten*
*scant 1 cup ground almonds*
*2 tablespoons flour*
*2 tablespoons orange-flower water*
*12–13 fresh dates, halved and pitted*
*4 tablespoons apricot jam*

SERVES 6

1 Preheat the oven to 400°F. Place a baking sheet in the oven. Sift the flour into a bowl, add the butter and work with your fingertips until the mixture resembles fine bread crumbs. Add the egg and a tablespoon of cold water, then work to a smooth dough.

2 Roll out the pastry on a lightly floured surface and use to line an 8-inch tart pan. Prick the base with a fork, then chill until needed.

3 To make the filling, cream the butter and sugar until light, then beat in the egg. Stir in the ground almonds, flour and 1 tablespoon of the orange-flower water, mixing well.

4 Spread the mixture evenly over the base of the pastry shell. Arrange the dates, cut side down, on the almond mixture. Bake on the hot baking sheet for 10–15 minutes, then reduce the heat to 350°F. Bake for another 15–20 minutes until light golden and set.

5 Transfer the tart to a rack to cool. Gently heat the apricot jam, then strain. Add the remaining orange-flower water.

6 Brush the tart with the jam and serve at room temperature.

# INDEX